Table of Contents

Dedication

Foreword

Introduction

Chapter 1 – Dick Pics Are Horrifying - pg 9

Chapter 2 – Anal Prep - pg 19

Chapter 3 – Some men – Suck! - pg 29

Chapter 4 – Ghana - pg 53

Chapter 5 – Sex - pg 75

Chapter 6 – Social Media - pg 89

Chapter 7 – Porn - pg 101

Chapter 8 – Relationships - pg 127

Chapter 9 – No One Pays Attention - pg 143

Chapter 10 – Fetishes - pg 151

Chapter 11 – The Money Shot - pg 159

About the Author

Dedication

For my wife Kira, without whom none of this would be possible. You are my true love, my soulmate, and my world.

Wait for the Corn:

Lessons learned from being married to a porn star.

Copyright © 5/1/19 by Victor J. Cipolla

ISBN-13: 978-0-578-53310-0

Foreword

I just Googled "How to write a foreword," so bear with me here.

My husband will and always shall be, my (best) friend. Yes, we're starting this off with a Star Trek reference, but it's true- my husband is my best friend. He's also my teammate, my support, my hype man, my comic relief, and he gives me that good, good dick. Hey, I'm a Porn star, and you're reading a book about PORN, what did you expect here? Romance???

Good dick aside, he's always there for me. Especially when I've had a few scotches and come up with some kind of crazy project adventure I want to do.
Art Shows? He made it happen.
Clothing Line? He made it happen.
TV Show? He made it happen.

The point? He makes things happen. He's a man of his word, and when he says he will do something, he does it. So much so I have to "be careful what I wish for" around him because I will wake up the next morning with a hangover and a new business.

When my husband and I were dating, my friends and family would ask what he did for a living. I would tell them he owned his own PR company, and they would look at me with a puzzled look and ask what that was.

My response? Vic took the Sicilian "I got a guy" and made it into a paying job.

It's true! He's always "got a guy."
You need fashion designers? He's got a guy.
You need jewelers? He's got a guy.
You need news anchors, artists, comics, pizza guys, wine connoisseurs, musicians, politicians, judges, lawyers, marble and tile importers, models, gallery owners, chefs, stylists, credit card processors, Olympic medalists, football scouts, boxing promoters, audio engineers, actors, Broadway singers, photographers… (I have more, but you get the point…)?
He's got a guy.

You need hundreds of lemons and limes right before a wedding? He's got a fucking lemon and lime guy. (These are all true, by the way.)

And I think Vic's great at PR and everything he does, because he's so friendly. I've never known anyone with so many genuine friends. He'll talk to everyone and anyone. He's not afraid to start up a conversation, unlike me, who would rather hide in a corner at a party, or better yet just stay home in my PJs and be as antisocial as possible. I love having him as my husband for many reasons, but one of my favorites is the fact he'll do all the talking for me if I'm shy, which is almost always.

So when I started bringing him around all my Porn star friends and all the people in the adult industry, he fit right in. He asked questions, didn't judge, wasn't uncomfortable, wasn't intimidated, got familiar with "terms" and how the industry works as a whole, and made (many) friends. It made me so proud to have a partner that didn't want me to "quit Porn" or shame me for doing what makes me happy. Instead, he was eager to learn the industry that made me who he loves today.

Hey, you need a Porn star? He's got a guy now (and a few girls, HEY-O!).

Now years later, being married into the industry (you like that? lol), he's become quite knowledgeable about a lot and has given a lot of great advice to both me and my friends. So when he told me he wanted to write a book, not only was I excited, I knew he would write something that I agreed with and was proud of. When I read this book the first time, I was on a plane to Europe, and I couldn't put it down. I laughed, and I kept catching myself nodding and fist-pumping as I read it as if to say, "YEAH, YEAH! What he said!!" I'm sure the flight attendant thought I was absolutely insane.

Being my partner, he sees and puts up with a LOT. Not only is he the strongest man I know for being able to handle it all, he does it with humor and a smile (and, well, lots of eye rolls). Vic did a great job of explaining the adult industry and sex from a "civilians" perspective… as well as being blunt and honest. He says things I've always wanted to say but haven't had the balls to say myself, and I really think you are going to enjoy this book. I recommend a sense of humor when reading, or a big glass of scotch. Both is probably best.

And Vic, I am so proud of you in so many ways, this adds to the forever extensive list. Thank you for accepting my life choices, thank you for staying by my side when family and friends left because of being associated with me, and thank you for putting up with the tens of thousands of horrible messages (and dick pics) you get on the internet. I love you.

-Kira Cipolla AKA Dani Daniels

Introduction

I have been in every type of horrible relationship you can imagine. My other book – *Three Exes Ago* – will detail all of those...from codependency to substance abuse to serial lying to immaturity. Suffice it to say, I have learned a lot. As has been mentioned before...experience is a great teacher. Unfortunately, you learn the lesson after the mistake. With all that in mind, I am sure you will all be surprised to hear the most loving, monogamous, trusting, caring, communicative relationship I have ever been in is my current relationship with the porn star known as Dani Daniels. You can google it... I'll wait.

Now that you have satiated your appetite for curiosity you will probably be even more amazed to know my wife has not shot a scene since we have been together, has not been with another person since we have been together, nor does she want to. By her own words, she has tried literally anything and everything she could have ever imagined sexually in a safe environment and has no regrets but also has no unfulfilled fantasies.

As she has said, when we met, she was finally at a place in her life where she was ready to settle down with no worries of feeling a desire to cheat to explore something elsewhere. I was just the lucky guy who happened to be at the right place at the right time to meet my soulmate – the actual love of my life.

But I digress…the purpose of this book is to share some wisdom of what I have learned from being married to a porn star. Hopefully, it will help a few people and shed a bit of light on relationships from the oddest of places.

One last item, this is my first attempt at writing a book. It has been edited a few times, but things may have been missed. The tone is very casual and familiar, so it doesn't always follow the strictest rules of grammar. I hope we caught all the errors, and if we haven't, my apologies. Should we find more, we will fix them in subsequent editions.

Chapter 1
Dick Pics Are Horrifying

No really, they are HORRIFYING. I am not saying this because I am a straight male, have some form of homophobia, or get upset by the veritable constellation of dick pics my wife receives every day. It's because they are horrible. Truly nasty and seriously awful. (Yes, horrible, nasty, and awful are three words that mean the same thing…but it can't be stated enough.)

No bro, your dick isn't the ONE TRUE DICK, like some sort of dick version of the Lord of the Rings that all will bow down before. Most likely it's a mess and should be kept behind the zipper.

Because of my wife, I have seen more dicks in the time we have been together than all my years in locker rooms. You guys are seriously wrong.

Some things you should probably remember:

- If suddenly you decide to take a pic of your dick while you are looking down at it over a urinal or toilet ...DON'T. Think, for maybe a second, about that visual...especially since many of you geniuses have yet to flush before your Kodak moment.
- When sending your prideful pic of your manhood...DON'T say things like "I know you want it" "You love the big dick" "This is what you want BB" (As a matter of fact never, NEVER use BB for Baby).
- You can expect some form of a comeback from the person you sent it to UNSOLICITED that refers to your member as small or useless.
- Do not for a second think that you are going to be the all inspiring dick...she or he will have seen better and probably tell you so.

- And, do not for a second think it will be kept private. You send an unsolicited pic, it is open game to be shared share with whomever. Mostly to ridicule you.

As you can image, because of my wife, I have a lot of porn star friends. At no point have I ever heard them say "Damn that dick pic was awesome" or "Look at that gorgeous penis, I want it." All I have ever heard is "What the fuck is that" "Look at this pathetic thing" or "Oh my god, that's scary."

These girls literally work with the best dicks in the world, what the fuck do you think you are showing them they haven't already seen? Seriously, one guy's dick (Keiran Lee's) is insured for a million dollars. I guarantee you your dick is barely worth a used Starbucks gift card.

Have any of you guys actually looked at your dick? Do you not have mirrors? Have you not seen a porn dick? I have seen so many disturbing dick pics that I have literally want to write "Bro, I have a dick, I know what one looks like, and you really should see a doctor." Some of these things look like a finger after it has been through a salad shooter...a PINK finger.

And don't get me started on the lovely dick videos you send. Seriously, wash your hands, clean your nails and for God's sake, launder your sheets! Can you not see it?

P.S. cumming on your own stomach, NOT a good look in case you were wondering.

Please explain to me what the mentality behind this is. You are SO proud of your dick you think that anyone who sees it will run to you and suck on it like Hoover vacuum?

Fun Fact: it's fucking UGLY.

Most men's bodies are ugly and hairy with this thing dangling between their legs looking like a loaded gun with veins. Thank God, someone finds us attractive. Even the best-looking guy on the planet with ripped muscles and a body shaved to an inch of his life still must drop his drawers and reveal the saggy, wrinkly balls and a dick of questionable size and look.

So why are you sending dick pics? Do you think the result will be positive? Why would you believe that at all? Do you find it works for you regularly? What the fuck is your thought process behind this? Has your little head completely taken over for your big head?

I am sure you are thinking, "but Vic, you are talking to porn stars." They work in an obviously sexually charged environment and should expect that. They are turning people on for a living, and this is the price they pay. True, however:

1. It's still an ATROCIOUS idea
2. It's not just reserved for porn stars.

Having not come from the porn world, most of my friends are your average everyday folks. Many are women. And MANY, in fact almost all of them, have had discussions with my wife about unsolicited dick pics!

WAIT, WHAT, Vic? Are you trying to tell us that there is a ridiculous amount of men sending phallus pics to women they don't know through social media who AREN'T porn stars?

Yes, yes I am!

That is precisely what is happening. Every day, around the world, dicks are flying, Tweeted, Snapped, and 'Grammed' to unsuspecting people all over the globe.

Gotta love that imagery. Wake up in the morning, open up Instagram, and literally a dick is in your face, usually over a toilet with shit in it! That will wake you up faster than a strong espresso...and really make you just respect mankind. We wonder why women look at us with faces of disgust.

As of the writing of this chapter, Jeff Bezos, founder and owner of Amazon, and at this moment, the world's richest man is in a bit of a controversy. You see, Jeff has been stepping out on his wife with another woman, another married woman. And it would seem his marriage is now kaputz!

Jeff started Amazon with his now estranged wife, so Mrs. Bezos is entitled to half. Half of 37 billion dollars, which would make her the richest woman in the world and knock down Mr. Bezos to number 10. That is one expensive piece of ass.

Who here remembers the Eddie Murphy skit?

"HALF EDDIE, ... HALF!"

But let's forget that the woman he is running around with was married…to his friend. Let's forget that she has a history of cheating on men and trading up. By the way, at the moment, she is trading up to the richest man in the world…but when this divorce goes through there will be 9 richer men…watch out, Jeff.

But again…let's forget all that. Let's talk about one thing. Jeff Bezos, the world's richest man, sent a dick pic. A dick pic. And the National Enquirer supposedly has this picture and was allegedly trying to blackmail him.

Let that sink in for a bit. This is the world's richest man. What the fuck does he need to send a dick pic for? Isn't his bank balance his dick pic?

Look, I realize I am not the best-looking guy, and when I married my wife, I certainly outkicked the coverage. Thank God she likes older, portly Sicilians with a chrome dome. But seriously, look at Jeff Bezos. He looks like Uncle Fester had sex with a Muppet.

BUT HE IS STILL WORTH 37 BILLION DOLLARS!!! WHY, oh WHY are you sending a dick pic? THE ANSWER IS that no matter how rich, how smart, how sophisticated you are as a man, the little head out thinks the big head and pussy is a POWERFUL thing!

One of the first lessons I learned from being married to a porn star: Guys love their dicks, and they firmly believe that their dick is so fucking special that it will just make women swoon and the world bow down to their mighty dick. Even Jeff Bezos couldn't resist sending his paramour a dick pic.

That's just beyond incredible to me. At no point did a married man worth 37 billion (yes I repeated it) take 2 seconds to think…is this a good idea? Should I send a person who isn't my current wife, blackmail material? Can't I just show up and give her a deep dicking instead of documenting my stupidity for fucking ever?

Robin Williams said it best…God gave us a dick and a brain and not enough blood to run them both at the same time.

Will Jeff Bezos be a cautionary tale to men around the world? Will the words in my book make a difference at all? Unfortunately, I think not. There is no helping a man whose dick is engaged, and his brain is not. The stupidity will abound.

Let's get down to brass tacks here. If you aren't with the person you are sending the dick pick to…DON'T send it. PERIOD. No, "my dick is so awesome it's different than all the rest", IT'S NOT! No, "I know this girl is a slut she will like it" ...SHE WON'T. No...just NO!!!

Even if the girl says she wants the pic...if you don't know her don't send it. There is a good chance it's a guy who will be using it against you in the future. More on this later.

And guys, even if your wife wants a pic of your dick, BE ABSOLUTELY SURE, she really does. Default to NO, always. And if she does really want one...bring her home flowers, cook dinner and thank the lucky stars you found a woman who likes YOUR dick.

Let us recap. Your dick is not exceptional, do not send it to anyone and in the rare case your lover wants a dick pic of you...be absolutely sure it's real and then cherish that person as much as possible.

Chapter 2
Anal Prep

Yes, it's a thing, who knew? Around 40% of heterosexual people admit to having anal sex at least once. ADMITS TO...so who knows what the real number is because NO ONE EVER lies about "numbers" when it comes to sex. No one ever lies about sex, right??? (looking at you Bill Clinton)

However, in Porn, Anal Sex...well, it's like eating potato chips, you can't just do it once. All the girls in porn who do anal tend to do it many, many times. And that is most of the girls in porn.

Confession, I have had anal sex in my life with previous partners, but I have never thought of her having to do "Anal Prep."

You may be thinking...well Vic... what exactly is "Anal Prep?"

You see campers, the guys in porn, well they aren't built like the normal male. Must guys could fuck a donut hole without touching the sides, but the guys in porn....they sport schlongs...no "penises" here...SCHLONGS. Yes...it looks like a 2 lb. pork tenderloin or a baby's arm holding an apple.

What I am trying to say is that they are larger than the average dude. And with great length comes great depths...deep in that ass where a lot is hidden.

Us regular dudes aren't quite plunging the depths that these guys do, so it can be a bit more spontaneous for us...but not in the porn world.

SOOO campers to not shit on a dick, the ladies in porn ... prep. I am sure all the people on set appreciate this.

My wife has a TV show called *Dinner With Dani*...you can find it on Amazon...kind of fitting considering the last bit about Jeff Bezos (Shameless plug...many more to come). In the first episode...and pretty much in all the others...butt stuff was a topic of discussion, and, the Anal Prep routine was brought up. Some don't eat for the day, some psyllium husk to clean out, and my personal favorite ... Gummy Bears.

As the myth goes, supposedly, gummy bears are fully digested and do not leave any 'residual' gummy bear detritus behind. When a lady who hasn't eaten in days so she doesn't shit on a dick, starts to lose energy...she pops a few gummy bears for the sugar rush. I dare you to EVER look at a gummy bear the same way again.

I may have just ruined the pleasure of picking out your favorite color of gummy bear and enjoying that lovely taste forever... sorry, not sorry. Welcome to my world.

Now, this brings me to why I even brought this up...back to *Dinner With Dani*. One of our first guests was the always lovely Phoenix Marie. Those of you who know her, know her as the blonde bombshell badass of porn. A woman who could bench press a Volvo in a way that would still turn you on and make you cry just a little bit.

She once picked up a male performer and curled him (yes, like a dumbbell) while blowing him. I shit you not (every pun intended for this chapter), but I defy you not to find her sexy as fuck even if she could kick your ass.

Outside of porn, Phoenix is one of the most genuine and sweetest people I have met, with a heart of gold. She is a fantastic friend and would give you the shirt off her back if you need it. (No pun intended). She is also an EMT!

Imagine waking up to her giving you mouth to mouth...you would then have a "grabber" because you were literally given life's breath by Phoenix Marie. Or better yet...explaining that to the Mrs. "No, really, I was dying and had to have her mouth on mine."

She is also one of the brightest people I know with stories that would curl a longshoreman's toes.

ANYWAY...Phoenix has a unique anal prep routine. You see...the last thing she eats is corn...since the outside of a corn kernel doesn't digest. Then on the day of the shoot, she cleans out until she sees then corn knowing that she is now good to go. Thank you, Phoenix Marie, for the title of the book.

Why don't you all go have some corn on the cob now....with butter!

Asa Akira is yet another amazing woman who is seriously hilarious. Those of you who don't know her are missing out. Besides being an AVN performer of the year, she had her own line of hysterically funny candles. One was called 'After Anal' - let me give you her description:

"Forget for a moment you have been abandoned in a cold pool of cum on a sheetless mattress in a room lit by a lava lamp - close your eyes and let us take you to a luxurious bed of roses where the sky is always blue, unicorns fly gaily above, and money grows on trees!"

How can you not want to party with a woman who writes like THAT? She was also in a Family Guy episode! Basically, she is awesomeness in a 5'2" frame.

Asa sums up butt stuff better than anyone. On the TV show, she said, "Once your ass opens, it OPENS. Your pussy will only open as much as it's meant to, there's a limit. But your ass is infinite."

Kind of Zen, don't you think? "The Ass Is Infinite." That really needs to be a T-shirt. Zen with Asa.

So basically, for all you Dr. Who fans, Asa's ass is a TARDIS.

So anal prep... yeah it's a thing. And if you think about it, in porn, it makes sense. The joy of porn is, you know what you are doing when you are doing it, who you are doing it with, the time you are doing it, and exactly what you need to do to prepare for it.

For us, civilians, NOT SO MUCH. Anal is usually an accident and probably 50% of the time, a VERY BAD ACCIDENT. Most of us try to fumble our way through it and figure out what our partner likes, even when you have been with them for a while. Nothing is set in stone, and what worked two days ago may get you yelled at today. You have no idea if it will end good or bad or satisfactory. Wouldn't it be wonderful to know today at 6:30 pm when you come through the door your Mrs., who has beaten you home from work and isn't tired, will greet you at the door in sexy black lingerie.

You will kiss passionately, and she will, of course, want to put your dick right in her mouth...then, you will eat her pussy to get her ready.

You will then do precisely four positions, start in missionary, move to reverse cowgirl. You will spank her ass and finger it. Then, you'll play with her clit as she moans in the throes of passion...you will then move to a spooning position from behind, and of course, your dick is big enough to get in there and keep her moaning.

THEN, you will slide into doggie and as you do that you will pull out Your wife (having done her anal prep) will let you put it in her ass with only your spit as lube.

She will moan like a banshee and cum like a freight train, and just as you are ready to explode, she will beg you to cum on her face.

At this point, you wake the fuck up and FINALLY realize...PORN IS ENTERTAINMENT...this shit doesn't happen for real. EVER!

Besides...what fun is it if it's staged? It should be raw and passionate and slightly awkward and a bit funny. That's so much more fun than the above.

And if you are going to try anal sex...just go for it. Live a little and throw caution to the wind. Don't stock up on gummy bears or canned corn. I am sure you know how clean you are at any given moment. And let's be honest, any guy who likes anal isn't going to freak out if something happens.

But you gotta admit…"Wait for the Corn" is an excellent book name.

Thanks, Phoenix.

Chapter 3
Some Men…SUCK!

No, seriously, they do. It's really kind of sad how ridiculously pathetic we sound when talking to a sexy lady "anonymously." I put that in quotes because I mean on social media.

The comments my wife gets on her Instagram feed, in her DMs, and emails is beyond disturbing but also comical. She has actually created a file called "Dumb as Fuck" emails…and it's packed with gems!

Here are some universal truths (and by universal, I mean the universe I view every day).

- The younger the guy, the dumber the comment.
- The more draconian the country's attitudes are towards porn, the more misogynistic the comments.
- The older the guys, the more condescending the comment.
- Anyone proclaiming their devotion for an imaginary friend (by that I mean the religious zealots) the more judgmental the comment.

I am not trying to paint this as a picture of every fan. It's really a 30-40-30 rule. 30% are friendly, positive, and genuinely supportive fans. 40% are mundane lurkers with the occasional emoji comment or the "damn you are hot." And then there is the other 30%. Winners. Seriously, just really fucking appalling.

I understand she's a porn star and you think that this means you can be an asshole, all because she provides you with entertainment that you choose to watch and obviously enjoy.

Your enjoyed it so much that you HAD to follow her and say something. Yet, you can't manage to not say something fucking stupid. It defies imagination.

Here's a fun piece of advice…"DAMN GIRL, I KNOW YOU WANT THIS DICK"…pretty much solidifies you are the dick, and no one will ever want that dick. (Usually, they come with a picture…please refer to chapter one.)

Do you guys really believe that "I wanna fuck you" will get someone to fuck you?

Do you really believe "I want your WhatsApp number" will get anyone to just give it to you?

What is the color of the sky in your world…really?

You think, in this world we live in, anyone who isn't indeed bat-shit crazy would fuck some random guy? Or they will just give you their number so they can be harassed daily because of that stellar pickup line?

Do you guys have a brain in your head…or has the little head lorded over your existence so much that you can't take about four seconds to realize this is fucking stupid?

Yes, a porn star has sex on screen and gets paid for it. Al Pacino also played a drug dealer in Miami, do you show up at his house looking for an eight-ball?

It's entertainment. The people have all been vetted and tested and know each other. ONE MORE TIME…they have been TESTED and vetted, and all KNOW EACH OTHER.

This is their job; they provide you with entertainment to "soothe the savage beast." It is there for you when you are "randy" or "lonely." Maybe it helps you and your partner get in the mood or gives you some fun ideas.

BUT IT'S STILL ENTERTAINMENT. Sometimes they have fun and sometimes it's work. Some days are good, some aren't. Some days they cum and some days they don't. ALL WITH A CREW WATCHING, paperwork filled out, tests checked and BIG LIGHTS in their faces. Usually starting at 7am…not the time anyone wants to get up to drive to a set to fuck.

And, these girls are literally fucking, professionals who have the best dicks in the world. You think you can stand up to that? Here's another fun fact. With all those dicks around as part of their daily life, do you think they want to see yours?

When you are done flipping burgers and McDonald for the day, do you come home and want to cook more burgers?

I doubt it.

Neither are they looking for more dicks. They have no desire to read…"I know you want this dick". They don't.

Also, what the fuck is up with the current social media culture that no one pays fucking attention anymore? (More about this later.)

My wife moved to NYC in October of 2016. At the time of the writing of this book it is June 2019, and STILL, when she posts a picture in NYC, guys will write and say "Hey, how long you in NYC for?"

Seriously bro…SCROLL!!!!! She's been here for years.

Or another one, "Do you have a boyfriend?" We have been together for over three years and married for two. Our wedding pictures are ALL OVER her social media…how the fuck did you miss that?

USUALLY, these are followed with "I am your biggest fan"…Uuummm NOPE. Obviously not!

Not only have attention spans reduced to that of a mayfly, but we are now all too lazy to look back a few posts to check out what's up?

Let's work our way back to the types of comments. They are truly precious.

Yes, I am older than my wife. Same distance as Bogie and Bacall (considered one of the greatest romances of all time, by the way). So it REALLY takes a lot of intelligence to come up with, "Is that your Dad." "Nice of you to take your Dad out."

Wow, you really hurt me. You think that by saying that it has any effect on either of us other than to laugh. What's your next genius comeback going to be? "I know you are but what am I?"

I am a 52-year-old man married to one of the most desirable women in the world. We travel, fuck a lot, own businesses together, seldom argue, are best friends and have a lot of fun. Neither one of us likes to do things without the other.

But you think that your "he's your dad" quote is going to get you… what? Attention? Or make us angry? Or, are we going to just see you for the pitiable, pathetic creature you are who probably won't get laid anytime soon.

Go ahead…call me what you want. At my age, I have brought "I don't give a fuck" to an art form. At least try to be creative. Say I look like Mr. Clean's evil twin that got hit in the face with a bag of hot nickels. That I would respect.

And that leads to my personal favorite. "He's got money"….nope, I don't. I ain't broke, but I am not Bill Gates. Here's something for you. She makes more money than most of you.

She owns five businesses, is an established artist with paintings in museums, has a fashion brand, a TV show, and other investments. She needs NO ONE for money.

We don't need each other's money…and that's why we are happy. Learn this, campers … the money will give you nothing that creates happiness. Don't get me wrong, I would rather cry in a Lamborghini than a Ford Fiesta, but genuine happiness and real partnerships comes from friendship and the kind of sex that makes you realize that person just touched your soul.

That is not what you are seeing on film nor what you will get if you think that "Hey you want THIS DICK' is going to work.

But those are usually the young guys or the guys from the sexually repressed countries.

I get it…English is your second language, and I can't speak Arabic or Hindi. Taking shots at a comment like "show bobs and vagene" is a bit cheap. HOWEVER, some of what you guys say…I don't know if it's a translation problem or you are genuinely sick fucks.

One guy said he wanted to fuck her and keep his penis in her vagina all night long and never remove it. A sexual sleeping bag so to speak.

They offer money for sex…usually in ridiculous amounts they could never pay. They are all just sadly misogynistic thinking that their maleness means all women should just fuck them at their will.

It is a guarantee that almost every horrifyingly callous, woman-hating, scary, rapey comment will come from an Indian male, most likely and an Arabic male next.

This is not to say all Indian men are bad. They aren't. She has some great fans from India, and many have been incredibly supportive of both her and me. But guys, police your own. Look at her social media. We really need the good guys to give the horrid ones some shit. Maybe then they will learn how to not act like an asshole.

People in the U.S. beat up porn as being anti-women. But the places where men treat women the most terrifyingly have the least access to porn. Go figure.

This brings me to my brethren: the guys of a certain age. Starting a comment or email on a porn star's page with the words "young lady"…not so smart. Are you trying to sound like a pedophile, or attempting to be the most condescending asshole ever?

You are on the social media page, website, or email of a porn star. NO ONE thinks your "sagely" advice is worth SHIT.

Your life choices and priorities are already suspect.

Confession: I didn't know exactly who my wife was when we met. I had known of her but didn't really know who she was or how prominent she was because my porn-watching days ended a decade earlier.

I have never seen her porn, or for that matter, any of our friends. If you are in your 50's and 60's watching porn, God bless ya. But don't do the "Young lady" shit. You really are NOT in a good position to sound condescending, unless you want to read an "Old man take your saggy balls and your shitty attitude and go fuck yourself" comment or to get blocked. If that is your goal, then by all means "young lady" away.

Then there are the advice-givers.

You should fuck… insert any performers name here. You should do anal. You should do double penetration while standing on one foot in a pink tutu during a performance of Wagner's "The Ring" cycle.

The last one was a bit exaggerated…only a bit.

Do you really think they need your advice? If you are following them…then, their career is doing well enough to have fans and they DON'T need guidance from a person who thought posting "advice" on a porn star's page is a good idea.

Or my wife's absolute favorite comments. "You are too pretty for porn." This one makes no fucking sense. Do you want to watch a bunch of wildebeests fucking? Is that a fetish I don't know about? (More about fetishes later in this book.)

Keep your advice to yourself. Most of the time, you aren't doing yourself justice by writing it, and there is a good chance you sound like an idiot.

I know many of you are trying to be smooth…you are failing miserably.

And that leads me to the best of the bunch. The religious zealots who want to save us.

PLEASE follow George Carlin's 11th commandment…keep thy religion to thyself!

Stop trying to save us. Stop telling us we are doomed, we will go to hell, sex is evil, and Jesus, Allah, God, Zeus, or the pole in Festivus are damning us.

WE DON'T CARE!

Organized religion has been responsible for some of the most massive slaughters of people in history. Horrific crimes against humanity, and just downright stupid shit. I am pretty sure on the grand scale of sins that God wants to damn you for, fucking is on the low end of the totem pole.

Let's be honest, without fucking there aren't humans, without humans there aren't worshipers, sooo how does God not like fucking?

My personal favorite is the people who say Jesus will judge us. Here is a person who was the least judgy human in history. He is even rather famously quoted as saying "Judge not lest ye be judged" and you think he cares that we fuck? Or, that people fuck on screen?

This is a guy who was the first public supporter of sex workers, stopping people from stoning a prostitute.

A man who said you shouldn't forgive your brother seven times for any injustice done against you but seventy times seven times. Yet, you all want me to believe that he will keep us from "heaven."

That a charitable person, who takes care of their family and friends and is not purposely hurting anyone will be doomed to hell for fucking on screen.

This all coming from entire groups of people literally fighting over whose imaginary friend is better.

Do us all a favor, go talk to your imaginary friend and leave us alone.

Ok, that got off the rails quickly and turned into a massive rant. Sorry, not sorry.

Let's see if I can add a touch of humor to this chapter. Let me include just a few gems from the last couple of days. Yes, the last couple of days produced these comments.

Here is just a sampling of lovely comments from a few days ago. (Words in italics are comments provided by yours truly.)

"What's the procedure to book you for the night" (*Procedure?*)

All of these next ones are from the same guy on one post:

"ily" "Asss" "Squirt please" "Mwahh" "Come ill Make you squirt" *(All written as is… you may be thinking … Vic, was it a sexual post? NOPE… it was a post that said she will be using Cards Against Humanity as her Tarot Deck. It was an all words meme.)*

But wait, there's more:

"Can you make fun with me." (*Sure, how about fudge sundaes at Friendly's?*)

"Hi Dani u r so sexy nice tits." (*punctuation bro, it's the difference between…helping Jack off a horse and helping Jack, off a horse*)

"I want to lick your asshole." (*This was on a post that shows a group of us at dinner.*)

"I want u do anal" (*This was on a post that was a picture of our handicapped dog. Some version of this comment is constant!"*)

"Can you please take a picture of you holding up three fingers, I wanna admire you more with it. I'm one of your fans, I love you" (*Sure bro, we trust you aren't using it to catfish someone.*)

"Yo slut can we talk I wanna fuck you" (*There aren't enough O's in smooooooth to describe this guy*)

"Please send photo armpits" (*Really????*)

"How you like cook Manuel Ferrar" (*No this isn't a typo. Not so sure Manuel would appreciate being cooked.*)

"Remove cloth" (*Again, not a typo.*)

"I Love You Fake You" (*????*)

"the truth that you're a bitch." (*A real charmer*)

"I want to represent in porno movie" (*Represent what???*)

"Is that your Dad" (*Bet you can figure out what this post was.*)

And the gem of the day…

"I love you so much I want you marry me and also I want see you have sex with men and when you have sex I put your foot in my mouth also my mother and sister have sex with men I wish you and mother and sister have sex with men" *(THERAPY…seriously seek out professional help!)*

Just a few from ONE DAY. Somewhere, someplace, Noah Webster is crying.

I sent this book to a few people before it was published. I was told by one that "What I think is offensive and appalling is nothing more than normal internet behavior, especially for a person in THAT industry. These are trolls looking for attention."

It amazes me that ANYONE would use the word NORMAL to describe this in any way. Isn't this precisely what women have been saying? Normalizing this behavior and blowing it off allows this kind of infantile misogyny to continue.

If this is normal, we are in deep shit. If I come across as angry or just as a grumpy old man, who doesn't understand modern internet culture…GOOD. I don't want to understand that, I don't want to accept it, I don't want to encourage it, and I certainly don't want to pretend it's ok.

To wrap this chapter up in a lovely bow…some men suck. Mostly they just make me want to apologize for my gender daily.

My wife takes all of this in stride…she is so used to it that she is jaded, as are all her friends in the industry. SADLY though, it's not just them that are subjected to this type of fuckery. Most women deal with this kind of rank stupidity daily.

I have a client who does Executive Coaching. She has an Instagram page. It is devoted to her helping people get ahead in the business world.

No sexy photos, no thongs, no bikinis. Yet every day in her direct messages is some form of a stupid, overly sexual seriously inappropriate comment.

You got to wonder, what the fuck are they thinking? At some point, men need to stop living up to the lowest common denominator and try to not act like a Neanderthal regularly.

We did an episode on our TV show, *Dinner With Dani*, which featured the guys in the industry. My wife asked the guys what advice they would give to someone wanting to be male talent. Charles Dera said, "Don't talk!" BRILLIANT. The best piece of advice EVER!

Immediately, Johnny Sins, Small Hands, and Joanna Angel all chimed in and agreed. Guys will talk themselves RIGHT out of business. As Charles brilliantly added, "Everything you say or do will be held against you in a court of pussy." YES, IT WILL.

Joanna Angel is one savvy businesswoman who literally made her husband do porn for her company on a "deferred" compensation basis. You will have to watch that *Dinner With Dani* episode to hear the story.

Joanna says she will watch a guy show up on set and see a girl look at him like he is cute, then watch him talk himself right into the girl not wanting to fuck him.

This is on a porn set, where the people are being paid to fuck, and even then, with a paycheck involved and a job, stupid male bullshit comments dry up a woman like the Sahara.

Dude, do you really think these comments work? "I will fuck you so hard!" No, you won't…if you have to say it, you definitely won't do it. "Baby, your pussy needs my dick!" Do you really think she is going to look and say, "OMG, it really does!" No bro, she is just going to laugh.

"No one can fuck you as good as me!" Seriously, you make this comment on a porn star's Instagram? They fuck, literally, the best dicks on the planet. Professional "fuckers," whose job it is to fuck, get women off, and look good doing it. And you think you are going to fuck her better?

As mentioned earlier, one guy's dick in porn is insured for a million dollars. Keiran Lee's, a dick so good an insurance company put a value on it. And you think your dick game can compare. Stop, just STOP TALKING.

Sadly, we are focusing on a particular group of people. Many of her fans are fantastic, supportive people who stick up for both of us when the idiocy occurs.

We appreciate all of you and all the positive comments, and we are thankful for you every day!

Chapter 4
Ghana

Oh Ghana, you West African sewer of scammers, miscreants, and Dani Daniels' catfishers.

This is not just limited to Dani Daniels. Every adult film star we know, including the men, have multiple fake accounts of them, created in Ghana, by a group or groups of people using them to scam people.

The Ghana Romance scam, maybe you have heard of it? Goes something like this. Someone in Ghana, usually a dude, trolls through the comments and followers of any number of adult film stars and picks out the guys who look older and desperate.

They then use fake profiles on everything from Hangout to Instagram from WhatsApp to Tinder to message these numbnuts and proceed to take them for a ride. A ride that usually ends in the guy losing a lot of money thinking they are dating the porn star, the "identical twin" of the porn star, or worse "saving them".

That is the elevator speech version of the scam. It's way more sophisticated. These scammers are master profilers who know just how to get under a lonely man's (and sometimes woman's) skin.

Porn stars are great to use for this kind of scam since there are plenty of nude selfies online to make it seem like you are in a "relationship." They prey on older men mostly who will not likely know the porn star, and if they do figure it out, they are sold a bill of goods about how the star ran to Ghana to get away from porn.

Needless to say, my wife is one of the most faked people in the world. We have found thousands of fake Dani Daniels accounts that we report consistently. It takes up a lot of time. And it is absolutely crazy!

It's such a load of fantastic bullshit that it continually shocks me how many people fall for it. I am not talking about the occasional person here and there; I am talking about dozens of guys that contact us weekly and post on her social media daily about being scammed.

The problem is these guys don't post and say, "I fucked up and fell for a stupid scam." They usually threaten her and still think she is the one doing it. Most of the guys, when confronted with the truth, feel like idiots and apologize. Many become fans.

But then there are the special ones that just will not believe they fucked up, so it must be someone else's fault. Usually that someone else is "Dani Daniels".

Mark Twain said it best…"It's easier to fool someone than to convince them they have been fooled." These guys then go on a rampage…we get death threats, nasty emails, messages or, my personal favorites, the guys who think they are still talking to her and that I am the problem.

You may be thinking, "Vic, what are some of these stories you have heard?" Well, let me give you a few of my favorites. The names are withheld to protect the innocent, the guilty, and the absolutely moronic.

The Litigious One:

Here's a gem. At our office, we get served by mail a summons for small claims court from a guy suing Dani Daniels saying he wants his $1,785 back after being defrauded. He is suing for $5,000; where that number came from is anyone's guess.

Now, I am sure all of you reading this realize…THERE IS NO DANI DANIELS.

It's a stage name of a character my wife plays in adult movies. Suing Dani Daniels would be like suing Michael Corleone for being a mobster.

Even if you give the guy a pass on that, you have to wonder how he figured out where our office is but couldn't figure out that he was being scammed.

This genius goes to small claims court in NYC to file a claim, and we have to trudge down to the court with our lawyer and deal with this.

This guy thought he was going to get in a room with Dani Daniels and make her realize that she was still in love with him. He even brought his laptop to court.

He was expecting arbitration…instead he got a countersuit for wasting our time. He dropped his suit quickly when he became the poster child for being catfished and an idiot by numerous press outlets around the world.

And he probably realized if he entered his laptop as evidence, our lawyer would have been able to look through all of it. Imagine what he would have seen.

Again, you have to ask yourself, if you can track us down at our office in NYC, how the fuck couldn't you do a bit of research before sending almost 2 grand to Ghana to see if maybe, just MAYBE, this might not be kosher!

The Twin:

Another great one…A guy messages me and says "your wife needs to help her sister". I reply, "My wife is an only child." And here is how the rest of the conversation goes:

Him: No, she isn't, and her twin (YES, TWIN) sister is in Ghana and wants to come home to see her father's grave.

Me: Her father is alive, I just saw him, and she is an only child and doesn't have a twin.

Him: This is a picture of her with her mother.

I get this pic. It's a horribly Photoshopped pic of my wife from like 6 years ago placed next to a woman on a couch that looks a bit like Jabba the Hutt. My mother-in-law looks like she could be my wife's sister.

So me, being the ass that I am, sends the pic immediately to my mother-in-law with the comment, "What the hell happened to you? I just saw you an hour ago."…but I digress.

I proceed to tell the guy that it's not my mother in law, and it's a horribly Photoshopped picture.

His response: Yes, it is her mother.

At this point, I am at a loss for words, and he then says, "You two are going to be in DC at an appearance, I'm going to stop by." Ok…whatever.

A month later we are in DC, and this crazy fuck shows up at the bar where my wife is doing a guest bartending gig. He whips out his phone and pulls up a picture of my wife in our apartment and says, "WHO IS THIS?"

My wife looks him dead in the eye and says, "It's me standing in my living room."

Lunatic replies: NO, it's your sister Anneka.

My Wife: I don't have a sister. That's me.

Lunatic: Yes, you do, and you need to help her.

My Wife: Dude, I think I would know what my apartment looks like.

Another guy at Bar: Bro, I am a fan of her that is her in her apartment.

Lunatics storms out. Now at this point, you would think this is over…BUT NO…he doubles down.

A few days later I get a message again…

Him: I am sending your sister-in-law money so she can come home.

Me: I don't have a sister-in-law, and you will never see her, and you just lost your money.

Him: Yes you do…your wife hates her twin and is denying her.

Me: (Thinking, "let's try another way around this.") Do you know when this person's birthday is?

Him: Yes, April 1st, 1985 (Seriously, April Fools' Day).

Me: How can she be my wife's twin and be 4 years older than her?

Him: Your wife is lying.

Me: Bro, we got married, I know when my wife's birthday is and what year it is. It's on our marriage certificate.

Him: She lied about it.

Me: So, the birth certificate I saw isn't real?

Him: YES...here is a pic of her passport.

He then sends me a picture of a passport from the Republic of Ghana with a horribly Photoshopped image of my wife from the red carpet at the AVN awards…because that is always an acceptable passport picture.

Me: Dude, that's not an American passport, why would my wife's sister have a passport from Ghana?
Him: Because her family hates her and she lives there now.

Me: I was just married three months ago and around her entire family, and not one person mentioned a word about a twin sister. Does that sound right to you?

Him: They all hate her.

Me: Good luck with all that.

At this point, I just blocked the guy and moved on. But one thing I know for sure…the twin of Dani Daniels never came back to America.

The Psycho:

We have one guy who for two years now has threatened me because he thinks he is talking to the "real" Dani Daniels.

I have talked to the guy a few times and tried to show him that he is being scammed, but nope he really thinks that he knows everything.

I am a supposed drug dealer who paid money for "Dani's" grandmother to have a heart operation and made her sign contracts by drugging her up to keep her in the porn industry.

I don't even know where to begin with how idiotic this is.

Maybe let's start with contracts signed under the influence are null and void. How about at any point she could have just left me? Or perhaps, just listen to any of the interviews she has given in the last two and a half years about her career.

Or how about she got in the business 9 years ago, and we have only been together for 3 years? Or just that fact that you are a fucking psycho.

Literally every couple of months for 2 years this guy writes or messages me on how he and "Dani" played me and she is leaving to be with him. Needless to say, it's 2 years later, and she still isn't with him. Do you think that would maybe trigger an alarm? NOPE.

My personal favorite was him telling me he has all my invoices from my drug purchases, and he was going to the FBI with them.

Drug dealer "Bob" always gives out an invoice with purchases. Hold on, let me give you a receipt for your purchase…so that's one eight ball at… But even that didn't send off warning flares.

Fun fact: I am allergic to just about every recreational drug you can imagine. I am the only guy you know who went through the 80's drug-free. He has actually posted this shit on my social media to which my friends call me laughing so hard they are crying, about how he was barking up the wrong tree.

But no matter what legitimate proof there is, some Ghana scammer he is talking to sells him another bullshit story that Charles Dickens couldn't have come up with, and he buys it. The problem with guys like this...they aren't stable. And we must continually look over our shoulders and be careful because you never know when something could go really bad.

The Sauce Guy:

(Spoilers) This one is my favorite because it turned out ok.

A guy messages my wife's Instagram. Now those of you who know Instagram know that if you aren't a person's friend and you message them, it goes in this folder with literally thousands of other messages that you don't see unless you check them. I check those messages for her a couple times a week just in case. (Refer to the psycho above).

On this occasion, a gentleman messaged about how he was working on a project with "Dani Daniels" that would help veterans.

Side note: Both my wife and I are huge supporters of our vets, so this got my attention quickly.

The guy is a returning Gulf War vet who was creating a BBQ sauce and was talking to a Dani Daniels about putting them in sex stores around the country.

Luckily for both of us, I saw this message before he could get dragged down a path and lose both money and product.

I was able to reach out to him and figure out what he wanted to do. His idea was to bottle a sauce and put Dani Daniels on it and use some of the proceeds to help disabled vets.

We both loved the idea and started to talk to him about it. We worked out a deal with him to do both a BBQ sauce that was his recipe and a BBQ Rub that was ours.

Dani Daniels Wet and Sloppy BBQ Sauce and Dani Daniels Rub and Tug Cajun Spice Rub were born. Named by my wife over a glass of scotch. Come to think of it, we do a lot of our best thinking over a glass of scotch.

We put a bunch in a monthly subscription box we were selling at the time and now have it available on our website at ShopDDBox.com…a portion of all sales go to help our disabled vets!

At least, in this case, something good came of this scam.

Unfortunately, that is rare. We have been contacted by a ridiculous amount of people over the last three years that have lost hundreds of thousands of dollars.

We had the Dr. Phil show reach out to us about a guy who gave over 100 thousand dollars to someone in Ghana. Amazing that Dr. Phil found us in NYC but the other guy couldn't.

We had a guy give 50 thousand dollars to a supposed company to put on events and thought he was talking to me and my Mrs. That she was just pretending to be married to me so we could promote events together. The stupidity of this defies imagination.

We had another guy send her "gas money" and iTunes card to pay her "bills." As has been said in this book, we have a TV show on Amazon. Do you think she needs gas money?

People, use your heads.

My wife isn't in Ghana, never has been, does NOT have a twin sister. Her father is alive, her mother isn't in a hospital in Ghana. Her grandmother didn't need an operation. She isn't studying nursing in Ghana...that's just idiotic.

Why would ANYONE leave America to study nursing in Ghana? Doesn't it take about 3 seconds to realize an American, and a prominent one, with access to some of the best colleges in the world for nursing, wouldn't ever go to Africa to study nursing?

You have NOT been talking to her on Hangouts, WhatsApp or Facebook. She has NONE of those. The picture of her passport or any other ID you have is NOT REAL. It's a random photo someone Photoshopped into a bullshit ID.

Come on people, no one uses publicity photos and photos from porn sets for their passport photos. YOU ARE NOT ALLOWED TO…that's why you have to go get a passport photos done…they have to be a specific way!

Let's also take a moment to think why an internationally famous person would need to pick your random ass out of a social media site to help her out with iTunes cards.

Don't ya think she might have family, friends, or like the FUCKING U.S. EMBASSY to help her before turning to someone she has never met?

Do you really think she needs to troll social media to find someone to marry? And why the fuck would you argue with me when I am obviously all over her VERIFIED profile, and I'm trying to get you to NOT send money to scam artists overseas.

Yes, we ARE MARRIED. It's not a fake or for PR purposes. Why would anyone in the porn industry FAKE A MARRIAGE?

We deal with around twenty of these a week, report about twelve profiles a day.

You really want to help REPORT THE SCAMMERS. She has ONE VERIFIED Instagram account @akaDaniDaniels. An account for her artwork @KiraLeeArt, an account for the TV show @DinnerWithDaniTV and for her fashion line

@ShopDDBox. Her verified Twitter account is @akaDaniDaniels. One verified fan page on Facebook @TheakaDaniDaniels. And a public Snapchat SuckingAllTheD

SHE DOES NOT HAVE A PERSONAL PAGE ON FACEBOOK AND NEVER HAS!!!!

EVERYTHING ELSE is a scam. It's a bitch to get verified by Instagram, Facebook, and Twitter. WHY would she go through that hassle just to create a new profile to talk to a random person who makes a comment on a picture.

She has, at the time of this writing, 2.8 MILLION followers on Instagram alone, and you believe that she zeroed in on you and said "I am going to start a whole new profile just to talk to this guy who said I had a nice ass".

Do you also believe that if you whistle at a pretty girl, she is going to run up to you and say "OH MY GAWD. You're the Man of my dreams. Let's fuck!!"?

And here's the best part: just google Ghana Romance Scam and you will see it everywhere. Or better yet google Dani Daniels and right in the Wiki page about her, it talks about the scam! Or try Google reverse image search.

Basically, there are more ways to prove that it is a scam than there are ways to actually scam.

But hey, if you don't believe me, I am sure some Nigerian Prince will give you a million dollars if you just give him 10 thousand.

Here endeth the rant!!!

Chapter 5
SEX

Here is the chapter you have all been waiting for…sex. What's it like to be married to one of the biggest porn stars of all time. The sex is amazing…but not at all for the reasons you imagine.

You see, campers…girls in porn are ACTING. They are not just fucking, and the camera just happens to be there…it's usually a scripted scene with a director that calls CUT and says "Ok…switch positions" or "Open up" which means to open up to the camera not open your legs. That also means you are being fucked sideways, and that is not at all comfortable.

What I am trying to say is Porn sex is not real-life sex. Capisce! Sex…is not pretty. It's raw, hopefully passionate, sweaty and not attractive to look at. I have said it before in this book and will repeat it again, so it sinks in!

One of my favorite comics, Richard Jeni (RIP), used to do a routine where he says, "Only in a porno is the sex Minute Rice perfect all the time."

He's right. Think about it,…the makeup is always perfect. The guy is rock hard, they are performing multiple complicated positions in what looks like a well-orchestrated sexual ballet. There is lingerie that comes off perfectly.

Every smack on the ass is timed just right, and hits that delicate fleshy part with a wonderful sound that makes the girl squeal with delight.

And it always ends in the perfect climax where the girl takes it in the face like a perverted Jackson Pollack painting, and of course she licks it up like it was the last of the Ben and Jerry's rocky road ice cream.

Porn is shot in 4k with big lights, and no one has pimples. All the close-ups show flawless skin and perfect penetration.

Yeah, right.

Has any of this EVER happened to you? Taking clothes off is NEVER that easy…EVER. Trying to do it without tripping or getting stuck on things is all but impossible.

Switching positions multiple times without an accidental hair pull or mishap or a pause to say,…"Hey let's do doggie"…NEVER HAPPENS.

Makeup and all dressed up…that's only for the movies.

Ass spanking…again…there is a good chance you will hurt your hand, her ass, miss entirely, or be too hard or too soft.

And the funny thing is…none of that matters at all…if you are with the right person.

Confession: The first time my wife and I fucked, we were like two kids on prom night…giddy and awkward. We didn't know where to start or what to do. Now, at that point, I am a 49-year-old man who had been around the block a few times, and she is a well-established porn star, and if you were watching…you would never have known.

But we were so in love and so connected that we awkwardly worked our way through it and spent 2 days fucking each other silly. And it was awesome…it was a mess, and it was, what both of us admitted later, the best sex of our lives.

BECAUSE it meant so much to us. The raw emotional connection, the finding out what each other likes, the laughter, the passion, the falling into each other exhausted and cuddling up. THAT was what made it great. And that hasn't changed.

Meaningless sex is just that: meaningless. You get your rocks off and wonder why the fuck you did that. For porn girls, you collect a paycheck and go home. Tired and sore.

Sometimes the sex is excellent; sometimes you are watching the clock hoping to beat traffic. Sometimes you orgasm, and other times you are cold and waiting on the crew.

Basically, it's a job; and like all jobs, some days are good, and some are bad.

JP, the director at Kink, said on *Dinner With Dani*, "It's a job…it may have better benefits than other jobs, but it's still just a job." Absolutely!

Now, don't get me wrong. My wife is a very sexual being, that by her own admission, likes to be choked and spanked. She loves having her pussy eaten, and she enjoys shower sex.

But she also loves just plain ole missionary. Most porn girls do. When you spend your life doing acrobatic sex for work, just a beautiful night with the one you love, together in missionary, looking at each other and feeling emotion and connection is powerful and hot as fuck.

Let's learn a few things. Porn is fun…it's not real life. Many times, girls are waiting around for a dick to get hard. Sometimes guys have to be replaced.

Anal scenes can be messy. My wife, when asked what's something you should expect if you do porn, famously said, "That you will be shit on." Yeah, that right there is the reality.

Porn takes hours to film…and is edited, so you DON'T see the fuck-ups. Many times, the still photos of cum are Cetaphil …you can google that. In short, it's entertainment.

It's as real as the Matrix. It's like all other forms of entertainment…exaggerated for your pleasure. Brad Pitt isn't in a real Fight Club, Keanu Reeves isn't showing up with a blue and a red pill to take you out of the Matrix, and Dani Daniels isn't fucking the pizza guy in real life. (Unless I happen to bring home pizza that night. Because NYC pizza is fantastic.)

Be entertained by porn. Share it with your lady or guy. Use it to jerk off when you are away from your partner instead of fucking that girl at the bar that you will regret later. Enjoy it.

These are pros…the Tiger Woods of porn (Yup I went there) they pull off pile driver with the same effortlessness as you opening a can of corn. (Not so subtle hint at the title) They make it look easy. It's not. Look at that position and realize just how insanely difficult it is, but how wonderful it is to watch.

They have anal sex like it's a mild form of greeting. They give a blow job or eat pussy like a starving person on the last piece of cheese. It's a fantastic skill set that we should applaud.

But for the love of God…do not think it's real. You don't leave the movies pissed off because Bruce Willis didn't really kill terrorists. Don't think Porn is real and be upset when you figure out the Uber driver is an actor playing a role.

NOT an actual Uber driver.

It's entertainment.

Ladies…enjoy it as well. Find something you like…look up a scene or guy you find is hot, and watch it. It's fun. It's entertaining. It's interesting. It's also fake.

I am fortunate. I love my wife, and she loves me. We are completely content with each other and want no other. One of the reasons why, is because we both have tried it all. And we both realized that it just is so much better when you are with the one you love.

No, we don't bring over Porn Star du jour for a threesome. No, she isn't out hooking up with Johnny Sins on the side for fun. No, I am not watching or banging other stars. We don't want to. It's not our thing. We don't judge those who like that…it's just not us.

What I have noticed about almost every one of our friends in the industry, it that they just want to find someone who understands their job, doesn't judge them, and loves who they are…not the person they see on screen.

They may be a bit freaky by civilian standards (what they call us non-porn people), but they are freaky with only those they choose to be. They aren't just fucking anyone that comes to the door.

So back to what I learned about sex… It's not supposed to be pretty. Porn sex is not real. One more time for the cheap seats - PORN SEX IS NOT REAL! I have said it before and will repeat and continue to say it in this book. Until it sinks in!

Sex is a funny thing…it's a human necessity. Without it, we don't exist. It is a human desire, a want, and a need. It is the thing songs and sonnets are written about, yet it is also our biggest taboo.

I have always been confused by this my entire life. How did something so necessary, so fun, so needed, become so hidden.

What I have learned from being married to a porn star is, everyone wants to talk about sex they are just afraid to. Many friends of mine, who I have known for decades, have now decided to speak openly about sex. Not creepily, not inappropriately, but just in general.

They laugh about it, talk about my wife's career, aren't worried about telling a sexual joke or making a sexual comment in a funny way. They ask questions and have fun with it. AND, almost all of them now have better sex lives with their partners.

"WHY?" you may ask.

Because my wife makes it comfortable to talk about it, and she is the queen of putting people at ease and making people realize it's not a bad thing to discuss.

I have seen my wife do dozens of interviews as well as ten episodes of our TV show, *Dinner With Dani*. And in almost every single one, she preaches communication. TALK TO YOUR PARTNER.

We do…and that's what I learned. Communication is key. If you can't talk to your partner, find a new one. It will NEVER work, and you will have problems.

You're miserable because you haven't had sex in two weeks…SAY SOMETHING.

You want some romance and flowers…open your mouth.

You want a spanking and handcuffs…BUY THEM and say…"Hey honey, let's have fun!"

Sex is what you make of it. It doesn't always have to be acrobatic.

Fun Fact: almost every porn star I know when asked what their favorite position is…for real (not for PR) they all say missionary. WHY? Because it's the most intimate and authentic.

They have acrobatic sex 20 times a month. They want a real connection with their partner and they most all of them choose missionary to achieve that!

Partnerships are a two-way street. My wife does something no other partner ever did for me…she takes me out on dates. Imagine that. Instead of waiting for it, you act. My wife likes flowers she gets them every week, I love lingerie, I get that every week. We both have fun doing stuff for the other. **EQUALLY!**

Ladies, you know what your man likes…DO IT. Suck his dick in lingerie like there is a diamond at the bottom. Men, cut the crap, and buy some flowers and do the laundry, eat pussy…like your life depended on it. Throw in a good ass eating, like its groceries, and live your best life! Figure out a way to enjoy each other again. I guarantee you, you can find it with communication.

As I said, many of our friends are now realizing that talking about sex is fun and talking about it with your partner is more fun. And, dealing with it, so it doesn't turn into a lousy hotel moment at the Commack Motor Inn that will only send you to Bezos land, is the most important lesson.

(If you were hoping for a more salacious description of sex with all kinds of details about positions and kinky things…sorry. That kind of stuff you can find on Pornhub)

Let me add one more essential item…CONSENT. Don't assume you know what your partner wants. Don't jam your dick in her ass and think it will go well. Don't stick your finger in your guy's ass without checking to see if they are into that.

Communication is critical, and if you realize you are freaky and they are as exciting as boiled eggs, you either have to work it out or move on. Do NOT ever, assume consent. The actual consent of your partner is vital!

So, lets recap: Sex is not bad, we should talk about it, and fuck your partners like it was the last day on earth.

Chapter 6
Social Media

Social media…if there were ever a definition of a necessary evil, it's social media. Instagram, Facebook, Twitter, YouTube, Tumblr, etcetera, etcetera, etcetera. Our lives are inundated with constants posts, memes, videos, pictures, comments, and other assorted social media mentions.

Porn stars can't engage in "traditional" advertising methods, as you can imagine why. They live and die by social media. Back to the early days of the web, porn stars have taken advantage of this medium to its fullest.

From the world of chat rooms and emails to modern Instagram and Tweets. Porn stars have used this direct method to reach their consumers because, frankly, there is no other way to reach them.

They have become experts at marketing on social media. There is a catch: trying NOT to get deleted by social media platforms for whatever bug they may have up their collective asses at any time.

Sadly, this happens a lot. Girls and guys are deleted continuously for posts that are less than what you would see on any Kardashian's social media, just because of their profession.

Here's the rub: scam artists, as referred to in the Ghana chapter, use my wife's and other porn stars' pictures to start up all kind of social media accounts from Instagram to Tinder and then scam the fuck out of tens of thousands of people. They also will report the real performers' accounts so they get taken down and they can now claim to be them. Pretty sinister.

And, the social media companies do nothing to help us shut these accounts down. But God forbid you show a nipple, they lose their ever-loving mind.

Goes back to what I said about the taboo of sex. Like somehow if some 13-year-old sees a nipple, the world will end in a fiery storm of brimstone and lava, but preying on a bunch of lonely men and women for hundreds of thousands of dollars….well, that's no big deal.

But I digress…we will get back to that in a bit.

Social media is an interesting look at a vast global community of voyeurs and self-promoters who all gather together in a shared space for the sole purpose of peacocking their lives to an entire group of people who have been trained, by the internet, into believing instant gratification is a real thing.

I think it was Stephen King who said: "you wouldn't believe how long it took me to be an overnight success." But we all believe now with social media, we are one post away from being a star!

Hey, we are all guilty of it. I have done my share of posting and checking to see how my posts are doing.

Being married to a porn star gives me a more in-depth look down the rabbit hole that is social media. At the writing of this chapter, my wife has 2.8 million followers on Instagram, 598k on Twitter, and 80k on YouTube. That's a lot of people.

For comparison, that is greater than the population of 20 of the states in the U.S. It's about the population of Berlin and larger than the populations of Paris and Rome.

I get to see social media in all its fantastic glory every day…and man, is it crazy. I am always amazed at what people are willing to write, knowing that 2.8 million people will read it. One could be your mother. Or, do they not realize that someone could figure out who they are?

That's like people who get into porn thinking their family won't find out. Yes, they will. PERIOD.

And, yes, people will see your comments. We have friends who literally live for the comments on my wife's social media. One of them draws herself a bath, gets a glass of wine, and reads the comments while enjoying her soak.

And here is why…yet another smattering of today's lovely posts. These on a picture of my wife playing pool with my daughter. (Once again commentary in italics provided by me)

"How far can that stick go up." (*I don't know Bro bend over and let's find out*)

"Will you marry me." (*Of course, that's the way this works you just marry whoever asks*)

"I love you." (*I know*)

"The best porn actress." (*Thanks I think*)

"My dick is hard for you." (*Lovely Visual*)

"I love you beautiful and I follow all my videos you a wonderful body I love you" (SIC) *(Descriptive)*

"Love Sex." *(Sugar Magic?)*

"Can I pls ask her out." (SIC) (*Fuck no!*)

"Fitness good." (*I pick things up, I put things down*)

"Don't hide I need it so beautiful right now im hard and ready for you" (SIC) (*Can you just picture this guy lying on a bearskin rug, tiny dick in his hand, smirking, doused in Old Spice?*)

"Do another armpit video." (*Why?*)

And about 50 posts of just eggplant emojis

It amazes me what people will say on social media every day. Many hide behind "private" profiles, but that doesn't mean anything. It's not hard to find out who they are and, if one of their friends or family is also following, they will see it. It's truly amazing.

I have learned a lot more about social media from my relationship than I ever did working in it for the last ten years.

I am always amazed at how many people see it and pay attention to it.

We are continually stopped by fans. I am bewildered by how many people know everything we do. Yes, a lot is posted. But they all follow to the point of knowing about our trips, what operas we went to, what happened the night before on Snapchat or Instagram stories.

It's a conundrum. (I had to use that word, it's my wife's favorite).

We do post a lot…my wife especially. She needs to, it's literally her job. We are careful to respect our family's privacy and keep most of them out of pictures. My daughter is a regular in my wife's post, but that is because she was literally her roadie and one of her best friends. We keep out family that doesn't want to be in posts and those who shouldn't be. We try to stay positive and fun on there.

We post a lot of travel pictures and pictures of our dogs (who are the real celebrities).

Those of you who follow my wife knows she likes to torture me on her Snap and Instagram stories, and that goes over well. Unfortunately for me. Many a time I am bombarded by questions and funny comments. Our friends love it, and so do most of her fans.

It's a lot of work to keep that up, and obviously millions are watching. So much so that I was asked for MY autograph at the AVN awards. To which I responded, "Are you fucking serious?"

Social media is the fulfillment of Andy Warhol's prophecy that in the future, "everyone will be famous for 15 minutes".

Now you can be Instafamous in your own world, or in many cases your own mind, with posting on social media.

Here are some fun facts for you to chew on about social media from Pew Research:

- For context, as of January 2019, total worldwide population is 7.7 billion
- The internet has 4.2 billion users
- There are 3.397 billion active social media users
- On average, people have 5.54 social media accounts
- The average daily time spent on social is 116 minutes a day
- 91% of retail brands use 2 or more social media channels
- 81% of all small and medium businesses use some kind of social platform
- Social media users grew by 320 million between Sept 2017 and Oct 2018. That works out at a new social media user every 10 seconds.
- Facebook Messenger and WhatsApp handle 60 billion messages a day

- When asked 81% of teenagers felt social media has a positive effect on their lives

In the U.S., 70% of the adult populations use some form of social media to engage with news contents, share information, entertain themselves, and post dumb ass comments.

That's about 200 million people in the U.S. alone. That's adults. Those over 18. That doesn't include the population UNDER 18.

That's a lot of people trying to impress one another. It's also a lot of influence.

Currently, the top 25 adult film stars on Instagram have a combined total of 70 million followers. Thank God no one watches porn.

I know you are thinking, "But Vic, what about overlap?" Yes, I am sure there is overlap. But even if it's 60%, that means 28 million unique users, and that's just on Instagram and only the top 25 girls.

It's incredible how few people watch porn compared to how many people follow porn stars. Pornhub had 7.9 Billion hits yes BILLION with a B (Right now, those of you old enough to remember have Carl Sagan in your head saying "Bullions and Bullions")

And NO ONE watches porn. Incredible. Like 3 guys somewhere hit refresh 2.6 billion times and must have created 8 million profiles.

Once again, I am baffled by the issue. I get that flat-out porn, Penthouse style nudity, and up-close pictures of nude genitalia should probably be banned on social media. But I am watching girls get their Instagrams deleted for an image in a thong bikini.

You have to ask, why? What is it about a woman acting sexual that is a problem? Could it be that this is the ONLY place in society where women hold the edge? The only two places that women are paid more SIGNIFICANTLY than men is modeling and porn.

And isn't it interesting that both of those LEGAL businesses get the most shit from society? They get shit from men, who realize they think with their dicks and realize woman can control them that way (refer back to Jeff Bezos) and from feminists who instead should be preaching the power of women.

Instead, feminists are siding with tight-assed misogynistic religious nuts promoting pseudoscience and claiming "porn" is degrading society. Strange bedfellows for sure.

And that brings us to….

Chapter 7

Porn

The other chapter you have all been waiting for: Porn.

Let's get down to it. One caveat, this is not a scholarly study. I will be quoting some stats that are easily found online. Most of what you read will be, as the title of this book says, lessons I learned from being married to a porn star.

Let's start with my favorite stat. Marriages, where people begin viewing porn during the marriage, are 56% more likely to end in divorce. Sounds horrible, right? Mark Twain said it best, "There are three types of lies. Lies, damn lies, and statistics."

It's not really statistics that are a lie, it's the interpretation of statistics and the actual lack of people's ability to understand percentages and ratios that create the "lie."

Let's break this down. Here's another statistic. *Divorce Magazine* (Yes, there is a *Divorce Magazine*, go figure) reported that 30% of ALL divorces involve Facebook.

If you caught what I did there, you would realize the relevant point that will escape most. The difference between "All" and "People who start after marriage." All is well...ALL! And "people who start watching porn after they are married" could be 2 million or 2. The fact is in the percentages. For the most part, 30% of all is going to be significantly larger than 56% of a subset.

Do you hear the cry to ban social media? Did I miss that? Don't expect that anytime soon. Social media is accepted, porn is not. Guess which one is going to be focused on, no matter how much worse the other is.

Let's do a bit of logical observation. Could we maybe, just maybe, say it's not social media or porn that is a cause of the problem. It's people in shit marriages, where they don't communicate, that leads to them wanting to fuck outside their marriage. Ya think that could be it?

The lessons I have learned from reading all my wife's emails, and posts from women and men who are married or in committed relationships (yes, this is a subset) boils down to one thing. Shitty relationships have a lack of communication and in most cases, a fear of it.

Sex is so taboo in our society, and we are so fucking repressed that most people can't tell their spouse simple things like "Let's try doggie tonight."

God forbid we talk about that. Why would a married couple EVER speak about their sex life and what they might want to try or, heaven forbid, discuss how their sex life is as exciting as cold oatmeal?

They say that three things truly break up a marriage, sexual problems, money problems, and unrealistic expectations. Boil that down further to one thing in common with all: COMMUNICATION.

Porn is not the problem. But wait, Vic, what about porn addiction? Here is the rub There is a big argument that it's a compulsivity, not an addiction. But let say, for argument sake, it is an addiction. It's far less, practically infinitesimal, compared to drug and alcohol addiction. If you have an addictive personality, maybe it is possible to fall into an addiction to porn. For that small minority, get some help. As an overall, it's not a factor.

Back to the lessons I learned. Marriages that I have seen and have watched on my wife's social media and in emails and other fan interactions fall apart not from porn, but from lack of communication.

When your sex life is down to doggie only on Tuesdays that are prime numbers and a blowjob for your birthday. Or, the wife who is 40 and scratching at the husband to pay attention to her while he falls asleep watching the ball game and twice a month gives her his best 3 minutes.

When this is your life…do you wonder why either person turns to porn or dalliances with a social media "friend" to find excitement?

Do you think if porn or social media didn't exist, that they wouldn't find another way to escape the doldrums?

Necessity is the mother of invention. People have been cheating on their spouses since the dawn of time, it's not porn or social media causing the problem.

They are symptoms, not the disease. No matter how many symptoms you get rid of if the disease stays, you die.

Here's an odd thought. Watch more porn. Watch it together. Talk about what turns you on…what turns you off. Does that look fun? Do you want to try that?

Maybe, just maybe, make sex and conversations about sex not so fucking taboo. Maybe teach your kids this as well. Teach them responsibility and that the human body is beautiful in all shapes and sizes.

I mentioned this in the chapter about sex. I will repeat it and add a bit more to it. Our friends, who now joke and talk about sex, have better marriages. And, her fans that are couples, and have fun with porn as a couple, have amazing relationships.

AND THEY ARE ALL DIFFERENT. Some are swingers, many (like us) are monogamous but do kinky shit with each other, some try BDSM, some a threesome every now and again. BUT ALL OF THEM TALK ABOUT IT.

MIND BLOWN, you talk to your partner you get what you both need, and you fuck like rabbits, and you are happy. WOW, shocker.

And let's not make it so fearful. People won't tell their wife they want a blow job, or a wife won't say "tie me up" because they are afraid of what the other person will think or say.

We have been so conditioned to believe that it's all so dirty. We are afraid our partner will think badly of us for wanting to use a butt plug. That's pathetic.

If you have ever seen the movie *Analyze This*…there is a scene at the end where Billy Crystal is talking to a married couple that has obviously been together for a long time and is not, shall we say, in their prime.

The wife is complaining the husband wants her to "do things" in bed.

Crystal's character then says…

"Here's what I think you should do, Elaine. I would do whatever he says. If he wants you to talk, talk. I would get on all fours and bark like a dog. I would do whatever it takes. Smoke some joints! Drink some wine! Whatever it is, to get off on each other and be happy. I mean, come on, look at the two of you! Where are you running? This is the time to be happy! Life is just too short! Too FUCKING short!"

ABSOLUTELY FUCKING RIGHT. Great life lesson from a movie character. If you want to believe something in a movie…believe that!

Dr. Jess O'Reilly, a noted sex therapist, a guest on *Dinner With Dani* and one of the smartest and funniest women I know, has done extensive research on this and has concluded that porn can be good for your marriage. In a blog post https://www.sexwithdrjess.com/2017/11/5-reasons-porn-can-be-good-for-your-marriage/, she has listed five ways porn can actually be good for your marriage.

- Porn can help put you in the mood
- Porn can inspire you to explore your own fantasies

- Porn creates new roles for men and women
- Porn can open lines of communication
- Porn can be sexually empowering

She concludes by saying:

> *"As for the accusations that porn consumption results in sexual violence and negative attitudes toward women, the research seems to suggest otherwise. Cross-cultural comparisons of crime data and sexist attitudes actually suggest that the availability of and exposure to explicit materials actually has an inverse relationship with these outcomes."*

I encourage you to read this. And that leads us to the next item: Porn fosters violence against women.

In an article by Michael Castleman M.A., for *Psychology Today*, details research that shows more porn equals less rape. Please read this: https://www.psychologytoday.com/ca/blog/all-about-sex/201601/evidence-mounts-more-porn-less-sexual-assault

Here are a few of the key points from this article:

> "Before the late-1990s when the Internet revolutionized access to information, porn was available in books, skin magazines, rented videocassettes, and at the limited number of seedy theaters that screened X-rated movies. But with the arrival of the Internet, millions of porn images and videos were suddenly just a few clicks away for free. As a result, porn quickly became one of men's top online destinations, and porn consumption soared.
>
> If the anti-porn activists are correct, if porn actually contributes to rape, then starting around 1999 as the Internet made it much more easily available, the rate of sexual assault should have increased. So what happened? According to the Justice Department's authoritative National Crime Victimization Survey, since 1995, the U.S. sexual assault rate has FALLEN 44 percent."

> "UCLA researchers surveyed recollections of porn use among law-abiding men and a large group of convicted rapists and child sex abusers. Throughout their lives, the sex criminals recalled consuming LESS porn."

Crazy right. Men, who watch porn aren't running around raping everything in sight? How can this possibly be?

Stepping back to the lessons I have learned... I said this earlier in the book: by my wife's interactions with fans, the men from the countries that have the most draconian laws towards porn also have the most misogynistic societies with the most violence towards women. They are the guys who literally say the worst things on her social media and have zero respect for women.

Coincidence? I don't believe in them.

And another favorite. Porn is causing a degradation of society and a public health risk. The last one is precious.

Porn is a public health risk? States have passed laws declaring porn as a public health risk. Seriously.

Do you know what is a public health risk? BULLETS. I am pro 2nd amendment and can tell you bullets are way more a public health risk than porn. Bullets cause, you know, DEATH.

Somehow the logic is, it's affecting our children. Guess what, no kid with a pile of porn under his bed has shot up a school. The worst thing they shoot up is their own socks. Disgusting for mom, much safer for their classmates.

Give them shitty parents, a stash of guns, a bullying culture at school and violent video games, and now we have a severe public health risk.

But we don't want to talk about that. PORN…BAD. Don't you understand? A nipple will rot our kids' brains.

Give me a break.

In another article by Michael Castleman M.A for *Psychology Today* – https://www.psychologytoday.com/ca/blog/all-about-sex/200904/does-pornography-cause-social-harm - points out some of the problems with this bullshit theory. He states:

> *"Since the arrival of Internet porn:*
>
> ** Sexual irresponsibility has declined. Standard measures include rates of abortion and sexually transmitted infections. According to the Centers for Disease Control and Prevention (CDC), since 1990, the nation's abortion rate has fallen 41 percent. The syphilis rate has plummeted 74 percent. And the gonorrhea rate has plunged 57 percent.*
>
> ** Teen <u>sex</u> has declined. The CDC says that since 1991, the proportion of teens who have had intercourse has decreased 7 percent. Teen condom use has increased 16 percent. And the teen birth rate has fallen 33 percent.*

Divorce has declined. *Since 1990, the divorce rate has decreased 23 percent.*

Why would social ills decline as porn becomes more widely available? No one knows. But the one thing porn really causes is masturbation. Internet porn keeps men at home one-handing it. As a result, they're not out in the world acting irresponsibly-or criminally.

I'm not arguing that porn is utterly harmless. Some men consume it so compulsively that it interferes with their lives. They need therapy. Some women become distraught when they discover that the men in their lives enjoy porn. They might benefit from couple therapy. And to the extent that porn is a sex educator, it teaches lovemaking all wrong. More about this in a future post.

But the evidence clearly shows that from a social welfare perspective, porn causes no measurable harm. In fact, as porn viewing has soared, rates of syphilis, gonorrhea, teen sex, teen births, divorce, and rape have all substantially declined. If Internet porn affects society, oddly enough, it *looks beneficial. Perhaps mental <u>health</u> professionals should encourage men to view it."*

We could probably use more public health "risks" like this.

Are there some things in porn I am not a fan of? Of course. Some people shouldn't do porn. They are doing it because they feel they have to and actually do not want to.

Being a porn star is not something you take lightly. My wife in an interview once said: "This isn't like committing to bangs, it will affect you for the rest of your life". With that being said, as long as you understand and are ok with that, you will be fine and do very well.

Porn that depict actual incest and scatological porn are flat out disgusting.

Are there edgy parts of porn that might not be someone's cup of tea, absolutely. Don't watch those. There is a difference between criminal behavior like incest, that should not be shot, and porn that depicts a fetish you may not like but is legal, and everyone in the scene has consented.

For example: some people don't like BDSM porn. We did an episode of *Dinner With Dani* that talked about this. JP from Kink (the gold standard of BDSM Porn) talked about consent. Every person who does a scene for Kink has all kinds of safety mechanisms in place to make sure it's ALL consensual.

It may not be your cup of tea, but let's not judge it.

JP has said he canceled shoots because he did not feel the person truly understood what they consented to or that he felt they weren't in a position to give proper consent. It's interesting that consent is way more important in porn than in, let's say, Hollywood. Here's looking at you Harvey Weinstein.

Porn is more than just companies producing scenes and feature movies. Produced porn is becoming less and less of what people want to see. And because of that, porn is changing.

Eva Lovia on *Dinner With Dani* talks about how the current trend in porn is for performers to take control of their brand. More and more performers are doing their own productions or premium Snapchats and marketing directly to consumers.

Eva is a sharp businesswoman and is smart about her brand. She is a good friend of ours, and we always talk about staying ahead of trends. She states this may be the beginning of the end of most produced porn. She is probably right.

Even professional porn stars are producing content that is raw and less staged.

From what I have learned from being married to a porn star, people like porn that is not overly produced and a bit raw. A somewhat more accurate representation of sex.

It is becoming more evident that the millennial generation doesn't like overly produced content in general. They prefer

YouTube over TV, SoundCloud rappers over labels and amateur or raw porn over-produced movies.

But no matter what the porn is, it's not an informative production. My wife agrees with Mr. Castleman. Porn should NOT be used as sex education. It's entertainment, erotica, stimulation, and NOT AT ALL ACCURATE.

As she says, if a guy fucked her pussy sideways like in porn, she would smack the shit out of him. It's rare to see a condom in porn, and ALL Porn stars advocate using condoms in real life. They are all tested every 2 weeks and do everything they can to minimize exposure to STIs, something the real world does NOT do and should.

Many positions in porn are designed for maximum visualization and are not fun. And the pizza guy doesn't get his dick sucked in real life. As Dr. Jess said to me, "you would have to be a monster to let the pizza get cold."

So do NOT use it to learn about sex…it's fun, stimulating, can spark conversation and can give you ideas of things that turn you on. But it's not instructional.

Let's get back to how porn is "degrading" to women. Women are in control of the porn industry. Women directors win awards consistently, as opposed to mainstream Hollywood that has given one-woman an award for best director once. Women are paid more than men. WAY MORE. Women control the scene and do not do more than they ever want, and you don't see a lot of #metoo in porn…compared to Hollywood. Still looking at you Harvey Weinstein.

Let's look at mainstream culture. Have you ever listened to a Rap song? Kayne's latest hit, "You're such a fucking whore, I love it."

There is a running joke about not wanting to be a woman on a CBS procedural. You wind up raped, dead, raped and dead, or kidnapped, raped, and then dead.

Go to an opera and tell me how the women bode in those. Usually murdered by a jealous lover or killed in some unpleasant way, but to great music.

How about mainstream Hollywood. We had *Twilight*, one underage girl's choice between bestiality and necrophilia. Disney's constant Princess theme of "change for your man." Literature, *50 Shades of Gray*. Do I need to go further? I am sure you are thinking, these are only a few. Really, you can't think of many, many, many more?

And what about our accepted cultural icons. Jay Z and Russell Simmons are self-admitted former drug dealers. Call me crazy, but I am pretty sure those things are illegal and usually wind up with someone dying. You know, like, from drug overdoses.

Iced-T's a self-proclaimed former pimp. All we hear is about how they were brought up in poverty in bad "hoods" with missing parents and used their "hustle" to get out and become successful businessmen that now go to the Met Gala.

Honestly, good for them. I judge no one. They did do that.

What about a porn star? Similar situation. Missing parents grew up in bad "hoods" in poverty and turned to porn, which is LEGAL by the way. And now make good money, take care of their families, run businesses, and employ people. Are they respected? NOPE!

Once again on *Dinner With Dani*, Romi Rain talked about being grateful for porn. She grew up poor on government cheese and had to struggle to make ends meet. She stated that porn gave her a career and opportunity.

She can help her family, build a business and a brand. Employ people and grow. Romi is an intelligent, powerful businesswoman who is entirely in charge of her own brand.

Is she held up to the same standard as Jay Z, absolutely not!

Why you may ask. Because once you are a porn star, you are a porn star for life. Looked down at and judged always. It's inescapable. I am not expecting an invite to the Met Gala anytime soon.

Might we ask why? Is it because it's a woman-controlled industry? Is it because it is a place where women have the power? Are we that horrifically puritanical and misogynistic that a woman using her sexuality to her own gain is more horrendous than pushing poison into the veins of humans? That the guy who was pimping women is accepted and can become, of all things, a *Law and Order: SVU* cop on TV. But the women he exploited are viewed as trash forever.

What's worse is that you have a team of feminist and religious nuts combining to push this bullshit onto society.

Politics does make strange bedfellows.

Fun fact: Gloria Steinem, the self-righteous intellectually dishonest icon of feminism, two years ago protested the Pornhub pop-up in Soho, NYC claiming that porn is degrading to women. At the same time, Matt Lauer was being fired from NBC for the systematic abuse of women and praying upon many subordinates for decades all while NBC executives turned a blind eye to it all.

Did Ms. Steinem protest NBC? A prominent place where systemic sexual harassment and degradation of women was occurring…FUCK NO. Why would we do that, let's just play into the bullshit narrative about porn because that's easier than actually working to stop the horrific abuse that is occurring in mainstream Hollywood and Media?

I also find it hysterical that Ms. Steinem is on the side of repressive societies that are totally run by the patriarchy and constantly suppress women's rights. These are the places with the most draconian laws towards porn. You have to ask yourself why. Is it because this is the one place woman are in control…sex. Most guys will go places with a hard-on they wouldn't go with a loaded .45.

You have to ask yourself, is this the reason for such a hatred of porn? Men in control don't want to admit to their Achilles heel? And why would feminists not see this? Are they complicit?

You also have a ridiculous list of religious zealots trying to convince us that sex is wrong. That somehow, SEX is the problem. That perpetual bullshit beat into our heads from a young age that causes people to feel guilty about masturbating or fucking and "God forbid" talking about it.

This from the group of people that brought us the loving things that were The Inquisition, Priest Pedophilia, 9/11, The Crusades, Suicide bombers, Evangelical Sex Scandals, and so many other tragedies.

If you read the bible…people were doing a lot of "begetting" in the beginning. Just in case you were all wondering that's fucking to create people. For those of us brought up on the New Testament, Jesus was basically a cool hippie that just wanted everyone to get along and do the right thing, and somehow that got perverted into trying to murder the entire Middle East to get his cup. Kind of a far departure from the original source material don't ya think?

But I am ranting here. It's just to show how ridiculous the hysteria is about porn when there are so many worse things in the world to deal with. And much of that hysteria is created by snake oil salespeople using the easy target of porn to distract from their own complicity in the greater harm.

Here endeth the rant.

Chapter 8
Relationships

As I said in the introduction, I have had my share of bad relationships. From drug addicts, to pathological liars, to co-dependents. A laundry list of horrid. I am not one of those "It wasn't me" people. I did my fair share of stupid. Some of these were my fault, some were theirs, and some were a double down combined effort at the atrocious.

Along the way, I learned a few things, and it has helped me work out what I needed from a relationship and what I should be doing in a relationship.

And then I met my wife. Which made me realize it isn't just me who needs to learn from past bad…both of us needed to.

She had her share of awful as well. On paper, our relationship looks pretty bad. A 52-year-old man with past marriages hooks up with a 29-year-old porn star. I am from NYC, she is from Cali, and we come from vastly different family backgrounds.

But we work. We have our fights, rarely, and our issues …again infrequently, but they are never a problem for a bunch of reasons. And they are definitely not the issues you all are thinking. Here are the lessons I learned being married to a porn star.

Comfort is your enemy!

Comfort in a relationship is a bean bag chair you can't escape from. When you are comfortable, in any facet of your life, you allow things to happen that are problematic, but you don't want to upset that apple cart, so you swallow it.

When you are comfortable, you will slowly do less and less in your relationship because you feel like your partner will stay with you because they are also comfortable. Sex becomes routine and less frequent. No more date nights. Romance takes a back seat to basically everything. And then you wonder why you aren't happy.

Because you allowed comfort to take over. Treat your relationship every day like you have to keep your partner. Take nothing for granted and do what you can to keep your romance alive.

I get my wife flowers every week, I bring her coffee before I go to work every morning. I write her a note on most days if I leave before she wakes up.

She takes me out on dates, writes notes for me on the bathroom mirror, finds fun stuff in NYC that she thinks I'd like and takes me out. And she always nails it because she takes time to figure out the things I love.

SHOCKER, RIGHT? ... sometimes you do what your partner likes.

We celebrate every 23rd, our anniversary day. We look forward to it. We take turns planning the day.

When I am aggravated at her, I buy her flowers or a card as a reminder to myself that I love her, and this stupid thing shall pass.

I don't expect her to just love me, I don't expect her to stick around no matter what, I don't expect anything.

I make sure I put effort into our relationship every day. We talk, play board games, cook together, run businesses together, brainstorm ideas, are each other's biggest support structure, and we are best friends.

I want to do everything with her because I want to share everything with her.

When you get too comfortable, whether it be in your job, relationship, or life., you start coasting through things and start telling yourself, "Well, it's ok that the sex dropped off because I am comfortable and really don't want to go out a date again., "It's ok that people are getting promoted ahead of me because I have a job and it's not too sucky, and I don't want to look for a new one," "It's ok that I am gaining weight since I am married and she or he isn't leaving, and I like food no matter how detrimental to my health it is."

All of those are literally horrible. You miss every shot you don't take!

Having worked in porn, my wife values a real relationship more than most. She had to go through her career being judged in every relationship she has ever been in. Even in relationships with other porn stars, she had to hear, "What do you know? You just suck dick for a living." Because of that, she takes nothing for granted and works on our relationship every day as well.

Even though I say work…it's really not work. When you do these things…when you buy the flowers and go on dates and always court your spouse, it becomes fun and something you look forward to. You will enjoy your life more doing things rather than slowly suffocating in the bean bag chair of comfort.

Suck it up, buttercup. You fucked up!

My wife has had a lot of relationships with super alpha males who literally live "my dick is bigger than yours."

I have had a lot of relationships with the quintessential "It's fine" women when it's not.

We were both over that shit.

When my wife has a problem, she tells me. Not with personal attacks and exaggerations. "You men are always moronic fuck-ups, and you never ever clean anything ever," which we all know is bullshit. Instead, she deals with the actual situation. "Hey babe, you really need to wipe down the counters after you cook. It's a mess, and I put papers on the counter, and they got fucked up."

Here's the other side. Just say, "Shit, sorry, my bad. I will be more conscious of that." AND THEN DO IT.

I can do the exact same thing to her, and she says…"Yeah sorry I fucked up".

Say you're sorry, fix problems, and move the fuck on! You can hold a grudge for days over which way the toilet paper rolls out, or you can fix it.

Also, when we are really stressed from work and dumb family shit, and we realize we are sniping at each other for no reason, we literally fuck the shit out of each other, and then all is well. Stress is gone, we deal with the problems and feel good. Try it…it works.

Don't give a fuck about what's outside of your relationship.

We both come from drama-filled jobs that can infect anyone's life. Porn and PR. We don't let what is happening in those worlds affect ours.

We may rant to each other…then that is usually followed with laughter. It's not our problem, so fuck it.

I deal with a lot of dumb bullshit comments from guys. Most of whom have the IQ of room temperature. I can let it get to me, or I can realize I live a wonderful life and theirs sucks so much that all they have is commenting on my life.

Our friend who goes by the name "Small Hands" in porn said it best on *Dinner With Dani*, "I don't care about comments. You are commenting on my life…so I win."

A – Fucking – Men! If you are spending your days trolling on Instagram and commenting on how someone else lives, all that means is your life sucks, and that's all you got. There are those that are living life and those that are commenting on it. Live your life, and fuck those who are commenting. They are miserable anyway.

Try not to go to bed angry and leave the past in the past.

This advice has been around for a very long time, but it's so true. Deal with it and move on!

That's the other half of this. MOVE ON. No bringing it up again later. Solve it and leave it in the past. Actually SOLVE IT, no "it's fine" when it really isn't.

We are both good about that. We never bring up past issues. We deal with the now, not the then.

My wife has had to deal with this a lot in her relationship life. If she were right or bringing up a legitimate issue…it would eventually deteriorate down to "What the fuck do you know you are just a porn star" or worse "You suck dick for a living and disgust me."

I have had my share of shit thrown in my face as well, but not to that level. She will tell you; I have never brought up her past, or her career in any argument ever.

We deal with it, and we fix it, and we move on. Some issues take more time than others, and I will say she is WAY better at getting over things than I am. But we work it out ALWAYS.

Being Sicilian, I hold on to shit more than she does. I work to not be that way. She can be pissed, yell at me, I say sorry, and 20 minutes later we are fine.

I do so love her for that, and I am trying to be better about it. I am just fighting the Sicilian grudge-holding genetics.

Delete Toxic.

We all have friends and family members and business associates that frankly SUCK! They are toxic, drama-filled, and annoying. They ruin your day and guess who you wind up arguing with because of it. Your partner.
Let's just say it, the thing no one wants to say, but we all know is true: if the relationship with your friend or family member doesn't provide you with value, it's time to get rid of it. And by value, I don't mean monetary. If you don't have

happy moments or joy. If you dread seeing them. If they provide you with nothing but drama, stress, and aggravation. WHY DO YOU STILL INCLUDE THEM IN YOUR LIFE?

Toxic will permeate every facet of your life. I dated a woman who had some seriously toxic friends. They were the miserable type who were single but wanted a relationship, and all hated on any friend who was in a relationship.

The girl I was with hadn't had a long term relationship ever. They all counted on her to be the friend they could bitch to and would be miserable with them and drink and take care of their pathetic asses when they got drunk.

Problem was: she was now happy and in a relationship.

I have never been, nor will ever be, the guy who tells their partner they can't see their friends without me. Have fun, enjoy your time out. I will be home when you get home. Call me if you need anything.

She would head out with the self-pitying crowd, and they would attack our relationship in a passive-aggressive manner. Little snippets of bullshit, ridiculous assumptions, and generally telling her the relationship was "doomed to fail" due to their totally uninformed opinions of what they believed would happen in the future.

Needless to say, she would come home a bit tipsy, and we would wind up fighting. Most of the time, I had no idea why we were fighting. After a few of these nights out, it was apparent what the reason was.

There was really no reason for us to have a problem, other than poison pills being dropped into her head by toxic people. None of which had any basis in reality. In the end, it was the demise of that relationship. It became a self-fulfilling prophecy.

Toxicity is just that: TOXIC. You need to evaluate your family and friendships and weed out the toxic, or it will adversely affect your relationship.

If your single friends want you to be single again so you can party with them. Ask yourself, if they get a partner, are they going to abandon them for you?" Let me help you. The answer is NO! If they want to go out and get drunk and hit on strippers or pick up people or flirt, do you think it's a good thing to be around that? Again, NO!

Whether you are faithful as a bloodhound or tempted, it doesn't matter. Those types of situations just lead to problems, misinterpretations, and uncomfortable circumstances you don't need in your life. Ridding yourself of toxic will relieve a lot of stress in your life and relationship.

Fuck!

Seriously fuck. Make time for it. Figure it out. Fuck each other silly. Have fun.

It's the best stress reliever in the world. It will reset your day, your relationship, and make lots of little shit go away.

Enjoy it and do it!

Be each other's best friend.

Seriously, if this is the person you have chosen to be with. Shouldn't you want to actually, you know, BE WITH THEM?

I have heard a lot of porn stars tell me this. They just want to do everything with their partners. They are the person they want to spend their time traveling with, going out with, or just reading a book on the couch with.

Maybe it's because their job puts them around a lot of people in sexually charged situations that make them realize that their partner is who they want to enjoy their time with, outside of work.

I am the same way. I don't understand the need for "Guys" time…my wife is the same with "Girls" time. There is nothing wrong with it…but neither one of us sees it as a necessity.

I know people who live for the time away from their partner. Why the fuck are you with them? These are the same people who say "Ugh, have to go home to the ball and chain." Why are you with that person if going home is such a horror.

I love coming home to my wife. She makes me laugh, smile, and resets my day. It's a respite from the crazy day. And when I am stressed to all hell…she jumps me, and everything gets better.

We love spending time with our friends, together. We love seeing our family, together. We enjoy time with lots of people, together. We are a couple and come as a couple. If that's a problem…then you won't be hanging with us.

I find that if I am doing something and my wife isn't part of it, it isn't as much fun and usually I am texting her telling her what's going on.

And the same is true for her. When she has had to travel for feature dancing, she was in constant touch with me to share her day and tell me what was going on. Maybe we are that gross couple. But that is a much better way than going through life miserable, don't you think?

Chapter 9
No one pays attention

Seriously, it's an epidemic. No one pays attention, no one takes a minute to research, no one thinks before they talk. Ok, I am overgeneralizing, but it is a scary majority.

I briefly touched on this in a previous chapter, but let's dig in a bit.

I am guilty of being on my phone too much. Looking when I should be paying more attention. But, as my wife will tell you, I am actually very good at multitasking.

My wife grew up in the era of internet and cell phones. I did not. We do approach things differently. However, what I have learned from being married to a porn star is just how little people pay attention.

This is why Ghana scams succeed. Just read that chapter again. We have both posted about it for YEARS, she has done multiple interviews about it, the wiki page about her has the Ghana scam listed in it, and there are actually stories online about it, yet no one takes what would amount to ten minutes of research to find what a scam this is.

It's amazing! But that is just the surface of it all. Let me give some examples.

My wife has a massive social media presence, we have been together for 3 years, I am all over her social media. She does not hide me; our wedding pictures are on her pages. And yet, she gets constant comments asking if she is single.

I am sure you are thinking, "But Vic, maybe they are just being assholes and seeing if they can cause a problem." Well, you are right that a certain percentage of them are.

But sadly, most are shocked when she says, "I have a husband."

She did an interview about six years ago, coming out of a bad relationship where she said: "It's hard to date in porn." I cannot TELL you the number of people who refer to that interview. Even though there are DOZENS since then talking about our marriage.

Maybe I should have titled this chapter, "People only pay attention to facts that support their own delusions." Or "People only search for items that support their personal narrative." Or "This is why people think the Earth is flat."

Here's another beauty I touched on before. My wife moved to NYC in October of 2016. It's not something she hides. She posts about loving NYC and living here CONSTANTLY.

Yet two years later, she still gets a ridiculous amount of comments like "How long are you in NYC for." "What are you doing in NYC." "When are you going back to L.A."

READ…seriously READ. Take two seconds to look before you type a moronic comment.

I get that we are inundated with messages from a variety of sources regularly, but that doesn't give you the excuse to be an idiot. Take a moment. Read the post, look at a person's history before you start to type.

It's genuinely hysterical if you read anything on my wife's page…you got a chunk of idiots asking why she left porn, then a chunk making comments about how could she get fucked every day and be married. You got a bunch saying I am rich and a bunch saying I leach off of my wife.

How these possibly can coexist is mind boggling. But yet there they are.

Not ONE Of those statements is true. And if you read anything she wrote, or listen to any of her interviews you would know what's up. It's not a secret but then again why should anyone try to learn about anything anymore.

Hell, it's on social media, it must be true. Go look at the "interweb," and you will see anything you want to back up any moronic belief you may have.

My personal favorite is the people who have been scammed. These are crazy. Once again look back at the Ghana chapter.

Seriously, I have people saying, "dude, your wife was messaging me." No, she wasn't. "I talk to her on hangouts every day for hours." SERIOUSLY YOU DUMB FUCK...would I NOT know if she was on Hangouts for HOURS.

"I got naked pictures of your wife." Yeah, bro, you and 2.8 million others. "They were sent to me." Really, you don't see how someone can download a picture and send it to you.

Just pay the fuck attention, and you would know it's a pile of shit. But why would we? That wouldn't fit into the sweet delusions that we have created for ourselves.

Not to get political but fuck it I will. Most of us have seen recently (depending on when you read this) the considerable investigation into whether President Trump colluded with the Russians to influence the election.

Here is what happened…Whether Mr. Trump colluded or not. The Russians, having watched the current state of Kardashian culture in the U.S., engaged in a social media campaign of disinformation against Hillary Clinton.

AND WE FELL FOR IT!

Whose fault is it? Not, Mr. Trump's, not the DNC's, not Senator Clinton's, Not the media's. It's OUR fault! With just a bit of research, most people could have deciphered the bullshit. But they really didn't want to. They wanted to believe it, so they did.

Face it, we want to blame anyone and everyone, but really, we have only us to blame.

Skepticism isn't a bad thing. A few minutes of research with multiple trusted sources or at least different sources will usually uncover the bullshit.

But learning my lesson from being married to a porn star…I don't see that happening anytime soon. Sadly.

Chapter 10
Fetishes

Some of you fuckers are twisted! Fetishes. I thought I knew my fair share of them. I had watched HBO's Real Sex back in the day. Saw horseplay and food fetishes. Everyone knows there is a foot fetish.

Yeah, that ain't nothing. On the fetish scale of 1 – 10 those are a 2.

My eyes have been opened, and unfortunately, I can't unlearn this.

Let's get into them. And these are just the ones I have heard about from my wife and friends.

Armpits. People who ask my wife to show or even better lick her own armpit.

FiDom – Financial Domination. Guys (it's always guys, sigh) who literally ask my wife to boss their wallet around. Buy me what I want you disgusting pig…and they do.

Mukbang. Getting off on watching someone eat copious amounts of food.

Eproctophilia. Arousal by flatulence. Yes, someone asked my wife to fart in a jar and send it to him. I have no more words on that.

Scatological fetishes. This one is literally shit. Shit on a plate and send it to me. Let me see your shit. Again, no words. Well, maybe one…GROSS.

MILFs and Cougars – I know, even though we can thank American Pie for the term, MILFs have been around since Adam and Eve and Oedipus. But you fuckers take it to a whole new level.

One of my favorite people on this planet is Cherie Deville…go ahead look her up, and you're welcome.

Cherie is one of our closest friends and was in our wedding party. She also happens to be, by porn classification, a MILF. Not just any MILF but THE MILF. For two years running AVN MILF performer of the year.

You may know A MILF, but I know THE MILF!

But I digress again.

Cherie, on the MILF episode of *Dinner With Dani*, spoke about the difference between a MILF and a Cougar. A Cougar is a predator of younger men and women, and a MILF is an object of desire.

She goes on to say that most of the underlying themes in MILF/Cougar porn are that the sex acts are not the guy's or sometimes the girl's fault. A MILF is making them do it through emotional pressure, coercion, blackmail, or other nefarious means.

The guy or girl is going to do these dirty things, but their conscience is clean because "Mommy made them."

As she also states, it's kind of creepy and can get dark. But it's a massive fetish. It's one of the top terms searched in porn, and our friend Cherie works a LOT.

Oedipus would have a field day in the modern era.

It's also why there are 28-year-old MILFs in porn. As Cherie said later on in the episode, "How many 40-year-olds are in great shape and look fantastic fucking on film."

I have never watched a scene of hers nor will I ever…that's just creepy as fuck. But I can tell you, not a person I know that met her thinks she is over 30 and she has the body of a 20-year-old. So yeah...she's THE MILF.

Back to 28-year-old MILFs. Mike Quasar, a man I had the pleasure of meeting only once, is a long-time director of porn. He is also one of the most self-deprecating, hysterical people you will ever encounter.

Go follow his twitter...trust me.

Mike is also incredibly well respected by most of the performers in the adult industry. He is by far the director most talked about in ten episodes of *Dinner With Dani* and always spoken of with admiration.

After this year's AVN award Mike tweeted, "I'm going to ask AVN to add a category next year - Best Movie involving implied incest between a mother and step-son only 3 years apart in age shot in one day for under 12 thousand dollars. If I don't win that one, the awards are definitely fixed!!!"

Bravo Mike, you summed up MILF porn in the perfect sentence. And now all of you understand that fetish.

But there are more. My wife has had people ask her to spit in their mouth, show her tears, see the back of her throat.

Your guess is as good as mine, unless you are one of them, as to how this is a turn on.

On *Dinner With Dani*, the BDSM episode. Lauren Phillips said, "there is a fetish for everything, somewhere, someone is jerking off to the fact that we are eating dinner."

Damn was she ever right. Just look up the search terms on Pornhub. Some of the top searched terms this year included Fortnite and Bowsette. Last year…Fidget Spinner.

Those are TOP-SEARCHED terms. On a site that had 7.9 Billion hits last year. Go figure.

Hey, whatever gets you off, as long as it's legal by consenting adults. Have at it.

For a world that is as repressed as we are, there are a lot of fetishes turning people on who won't dare talk about sex.

And you've got to love the internet and social media. The great melting pot of twisted. If you have a fart fetish, you can easily find an entire group of people who enjoy that same fetish.

This is not something that could have been done 25 years ago. There wasn't a library of fetishes to see if you shared your particular proclivity with anyone else.

But now, thanks to the lovely web, you can find all those who are eating beans and living their best life. Gotta love it.

Chapter 11
The Money Shot

Other than writing over 150 pages to prove that I am a grumpy, sarcastic fuck, hopefully, you learned something.

Here is the biggest lesson for everyone to learn. Nothing is ever what it seems, ESPECIALLY on social media.

What you think you know is most likely wrong. What you are expecting is probably not going to happen, and all your "judgments" are crap.

Opinions are like assholes, everyone has them, and they all stink.

Fact is, I am married to one of the biggest adult film stars ever. What should be horrible by most of the judgy standards out there is the best, most loving relationship I have ever been in.

You should all learn this valuable lesson. Don't give a fuck what anyone thinks and judge things for yourself. Not by what your parents, friends, or the internet tells you.

Be with someone whose differences complement yours. I am an extrovert to the extreme. My wife is an introvert, and together we have the right level of social interaction.

Be with someone who shares your passions or is at least open to it.

We both love art and opera and have traveled to places just to see museums. We are both foodies and are willing to try things the other has done to check it out.

My wife got me into hot pot ... had no clue what that was before her, now we go regularly.

I love Broadway, my Mrs. was not the biggest fan, but since we started to go, she has developed a joy for it, if only because she loves the way it makes her husband smile.

She now goes to Yankee games and basically enjoys seeing me go apoplectic at the stadium.

I love sitting at home and playing board games with her or reading a book together. Something a few years ago that would have sent me climbing up the walls.

She smokes cigars, I don't. I don't care that she smokes, and she doesn't care that don't

We value our friends and family, and we both go out of our way for them.

I NEVER have to ask her to see my parents or do something for a birthday or event. She usually beats me to it. I am very close to her family, they are my family. We don't have "sides" we treat our family AS a family.

What does that have to do with being married to a porn star? It has nothing to do with it. What it has to do with is being a real person married to a great person.

What I learned from being married to a porn star is that everyone can teach you something, doesn't matter if it's a porn star or a preacher, a president, or a pastry chef. You can learn something from everyone.

There is value in all relationships.

With my marriage to a porn star, I learned what true love is. I learned what a real partnership is supposed to be, and I learned how to value that every day.

I hope you find the same on your journeys.

Here truly endeth the rant!

About The Author

Having worked in PR and Advertising for over 25 years, Vic is uniquely qualified to tell the difference between New Coke and Original Coke. Vic has won awards for advertising, written speeches for prominent politicians, and placed 10s of thousands of stories over the years, but he is most proud of the fact that he can quote *Casablanca* from beginning to end. "Here's looking at you kid".

Vic has worked as a publicist in a variety of industries from fashion to medical imaging; while always maintaining the ability to distinguish the subtle nuances in a variety of single malt scotches. A self-diagnosed coffee addict – he never sleeps, so he is always available to his clients, much to the chagrin of his wife at 2am.

Vic was honored to be part of the biggest interdimensional cross rip since the Tunguska blast of 1909, and once infamously tied a Marilyn Monroe doppelganger to a bed with a client's ties as, an instructional video on how to tie the perfect knot.

An Evil Genius, Vic approaches his life with certain aplomb reminiscent of the halcyon days of the Rat Pack.

But really if it weren't for his wife Kira, Vic wouldn't be nearly as interesting.

…And all this comes with a tiny drop of Retsyn© as well!

Printed in Poland
by Amazon Fulfillment
Poland Sp. z o.o., Wrocław